YOU
The Mail on Sunday Magazine

D1192877

Royal Photo File

It's been a great year for royal pictures. The whirr of the Olympus and the click of the Nikon have echoed round the land – and halfway round the world – recording every move, every gracious nod, every flutter of an eyelash as the Royals go about their state occasions.

YOU, The Mail on Sunday Magazine, is justly renowned for its Royal Photo File, vivid, intimate action pictures of the Royal Family on duty, at play or simply relaxing. High point of the year has been the arrival of the new baby prince, brother to William. To celebrate the birth of Prince Harry, YOU Magazine, in association with leading royal photographer Jim Bennett, presents this souvenir album of the Royal Year in pictures.

Bennett, a Londoner, is a freelance who has been following the Royal Family exclusively for four years. In that time he has travelled thousands of miles and shot thousands of feet of film. Before that he specialised in photographing motor racing and equestrian events – racing cars and horses need the same technique. It was because of their great love of horses that he began photographing the Royals.

Note for the technically-minded: Bennett uses four Nikon F3 cameras with 600mm and 300mm telephoto lenses and a Nikon motordrive FM2 for passing car shots. He uses Kodak Ektachrome 200 colour film.

Published by Harmsworth Publications Ltd.,
for Associated Newspapers Group plc.
© 1984 Associated Newspapers Group plc.
All pictures © 1984 Jim Bennett of Alpha
Press Agency, except as below.
Front Cover, Back Cover and pictures on
Pages 6, 7 © 1984 Lord Snowdon.
ISBN 0 85144 277 3
Typesetting by Cogent Phototypesetters Ltd, London NW6 6RJ.
Printed by Chase Web Offset, St. Austell, Cornwall PL25 4TN.

Off to
see the
new baby

On Saturday, September 15, 1984, at 4.20 in
the afternoon, Prince Henry Charles Albert
David was born at St. Mary's Hospital,
Paddington, London. The next day, sitting on
his father's lap, big brother Prince William
was taken to see the new baby. Nanny Barnes
went, too.

Harry
goes
home

Lady Sarah goes to college

At 20, Princess Margaret's daughter, Lady Sarah, is growing up. This means studying textiles and fashion at the Middlesex College in North London *(right)* – and learning how to park her Escort *(left)*.

It's been the year of the Royal hat

Princess Diana's taste for eye-riveting hats has revived a dying trade. And Princess Anne and Princess Michael of Kent are doing their bit, too.

And the Duke has an eye for a top titfer too

Diana can even give oomph to a sweet factory hat. She wore this when visiting one at Bridgend, South Wales.

The Duke of Edinburgh wears a topper with the same dash he displays in carriage driving contests.

There were solemn times

Princess Anne, Prince Edward, Prince Andrew, Princess Diana, Prince Charles, Princess Margaret – they were all there to pay tribute to a dearly-loved uncle, Earl Mountbatten, murdered by the IRA. The Mountbatten Memorial on Foreign Office Green was unveiled last winter.

A giant step for a small Prince

After summer holidays at Balmoral, Prince William, at two, decides he is old enough to tackle the aircraft steps on his own. But when jets roar, Daddy's hand is comforting.

Our Val at the Flower Show

The Queen herself is said to have christened the 39-year-old Princess Michael of Kent "Our Val" because of her striking, Valkyrie-like presence. But Czech-born Marie-Christine is settling in. The Chelsea Flower Show has become a regular engagement *(right)*. And she likes horses!

The sporting Princes

Cambridge undergraduate Edward *(right)* is good enough at rugby to play for his college. And he shares his father's enthusiasm for carriage driving, an activity that is notoriously fast and furious. Here he is helping to harness up *(left)*.

Prince Charles will try anything – including abseiling *(below)* with university students in South Wales.

Anne...
in rain
or shine

You win some, you lose some . . .
At the Windsor Horse Trials in May
it bucketed down on Princess Anne.
But the sun smiled when she visited
the Riding for Disabled centre at
Chartham, Kent, the same month
(right). And she took good weather
to the Save the Children Fund
clay-pigeon shoot with her husband
Mark, the Duke of Kent and Prince
Andrew *(below)*.

Flowers
for
the Queen

Wherever she goes, to church at Sandringham at Christmas or on walkabout in a Croydon shopping centre, the people say it with flowers – or a riot of flags.

Diana in the pink … and with the Pearlies

The Royal Family has few subjects more faithful, more enthusiastic or more cheerful than those other kings and queens, the London Pearlies. In the Pearly kingdom of Deptford, Princess Diana is presented with a jolly pearly doll by Nicola Conway, eight, at the opening of the Albany Centre for the Aged.

Below: On a hot afternoon at Cirencester, Princess Diana is cooler in pink than the man in blue in the background. Prince Charles was playing polo.

Happy birthday
to you ...

84 happy, glorious years

The Queen Mother's 84th birthday in August . . . *Above*: She leaves her home, Clarence House, with Prince Charles, Viscount Linley and Lady Sarah Armstrong-Jones at her side. *Left*: She mingles with a crowd of youthful well-wishers.

Right: Age does not deter the Queen Mother from attending great state occasions. Here she is on her way to the Trooping the Colour ceremony with the Princess of Wales.

Service
in the
field

As Colonel-in-Chief of the Parachute Regiment *(top right)*, Prince Charles talks to veterans of the Battle of Arnhem at the Arnhem Anniversary ceremony in September.

A different kind of field, but giving sterling service . . . Princess Anne lugs conifers around while helping her husband Mark lay out the course at Gatcombe Horse Trials *(left)*.

A different kind of service . . . the Duchess of Kent *(right)* joins in the carol singing in church at King's Lynn, Norfolk. Her favourite composer of sacred music is Bach.

She works for others, too

As devoted mother to Zara and Peter, Princess Anne feels deeply for children less fortunate than her own. She wore this snazzy cap *(right)* to help advertise her favourite good cause at a clay-pigeon shoot in aid of the Save The Children Fund at the North Wales Shooting School, Sealand Manor, Deeside. The Princess is President of the Fund.

Daughter Zara looks pensive *(left)* – and the family detective looks vigilant – as Anne and her children attend a polo match at Windsor.

Young brother helps out

When big sister needs a helping hand, Prince Andrew is there to do his bit – as he did at the Save The Children Fund clay-pigeon shoot.

Princess Diana in Norway

The Princess of Wales went solo to Norway, the friendliest and most hospitable of the Scandinavian countries. Diana must have felt particularly at home in Oslo – there she met the cast of the English National Opera *(left)*, who were also appearing in the Norwegian capital. The Princess planted a tree in the grounds of the British Embassy, where a small girl greeted her with flowers *(right)*.

Edward, the student prince

Edward, youngest of the Queen's sons, was 20 in March. He is in his second year at Jesus College, Cambridge, where he is reading archaeology and anthropology. *Left:* Edward meets the Master of his College, Sir Alan Cottrell, and Lady Cottrell. *Above:* Edward lends a willing hand at the horse trials at Gatcombe Park, his sister's Gloucestershire home, in September. *Right:* Edward enjoying himself at the Ascot Fair.

Never far from the thunder of hooves

Royalty's affinity with horses is enduring, whether the occasion is a sporting one, a family outing, or one of State.

Left: Prince Philip sets out on a carriage drive at Windsor.

Above: The Duke and his youngest son, Edward, at Ascot Fair.

Right: Prince Charles prepares for a polo tournament at Windsor.

Lady in waiting

One of the Princess of Wales's last public outings before having her baby. She and the Prince of Wales flew by helicopter to Salisbury, Wiltshire, for the opening of a special unit for the disabled set up at the Quantock Hospital.

Right: Prince Charles mingles with well-wishers. Somewhere on the way he has acquired a flower for his button-hole.

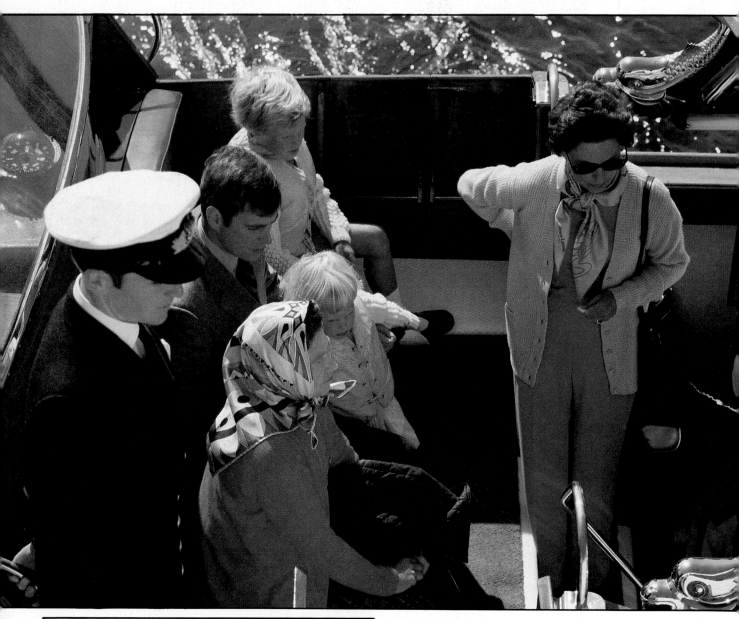

Let's call in on Grandma ...

The Royal Family's summer break is always a lively affair. It can be quite rugged, too. Peter and Zara Phillips had to wear life-jackets when they joined the Queen, Prince Andrew and Princess Margaret on board a launch bound for the Castle of Mey, the Queen Mother's remote summer refuge in the far north of Scotland.

Left: Zara Phillips looking pleased with herself at Windsor. *Right:* Zara and Peter stealing the show, as they usually do, at Badminton.

Getting away from it all

If anyone is entitled to a holiday, it is the hard-working Royals. *Left:* Christmas at Sandringham, and the Duchess of Kent wears a seasonal jumper to keep out the cold.

Right: Charles and Diana on the ski slopes of Vaduz in Liechtenstein.

Below: With a lady-in-waiting and a faithful corgi for company, the Queen Mother strolls on a Norfolk beach.

A Queen and two loyal subjects

This solitary figure on an empty Norfolk beach could be almost anyone. The corgis provide a clue to her identity . . . the Queen on holiday at her Sandringham home.

Future king and the best loved Great Grannie in the land

Royal
Photo
File

YOU
The Mail on Sunday Magazine

Prince Harry Official Pictures

£1.50